I Love You Forever and a Day

Mother and Daughter

Written and Illustrated by
Brandi L. McMahan

One night
a girl said to
her mother...

Mommy,
I don't
ever
want
you
to be
sad.

to which she replied

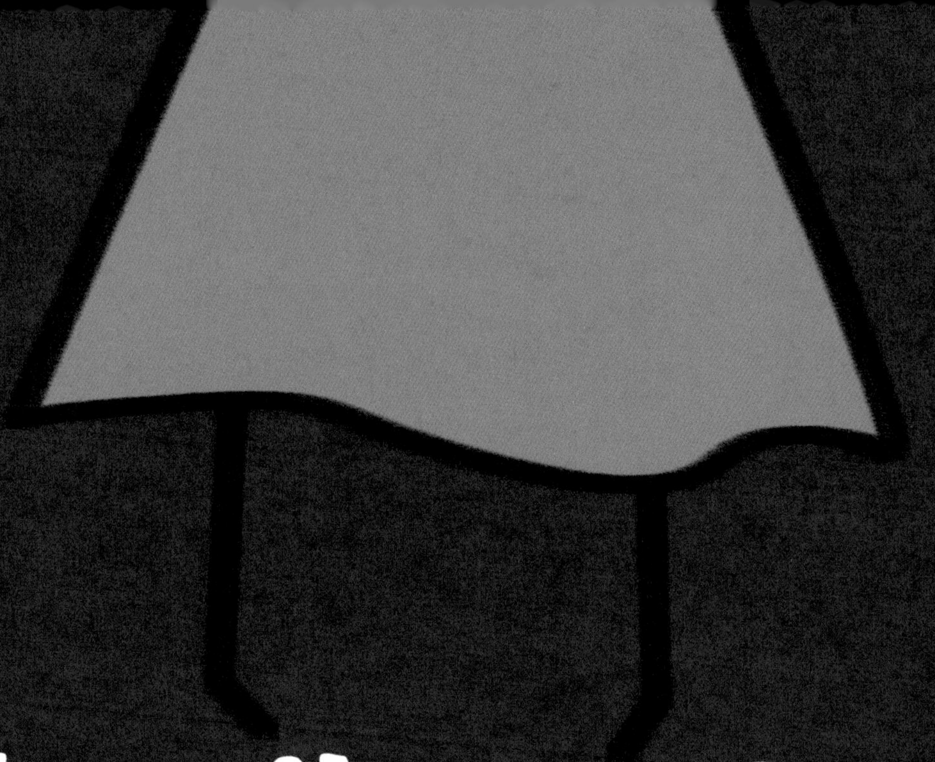

I can't promise that I'll *never* be sad

but sometimes even when I am....

...I promise

I still

love

you!

Then
she went on
to say...

I love you
every hour...

of **every** day!

and every minute

between

I love you in the morning

and I
love you
at night

...and every day

Wednesday

Tuesday

Thursday

Monday

Friday

of the week

I love you on

Monday

Tuesday

and Wednesday too

I love you EVERY

...and especially
on Saturday

On Sunday

I love you
even more!

I love you Dear

all through the year

every month

IT'S TRUE

I love you in January
and in February
I really truly DO!

I love you in March
and in April

then, come May
I Love You
GREATER!

I love you in June, July and in August

In September, October and November

I LOVE YOU
all the way til
December

I Love You

Forever
and a Day

from beginning

to end

I love you
my sweetheart

My FOREVER
friend!

THE END

for my Breckin...

My beautiful niece inside and out!

Love Aunt B!

Made in the USA
Monee, IL
28 November 2021